WOULD YOU LIKE FREE RESOURCES?

EMAIL "FREE" TO DECODABLETEXTS@GMAIL.COM TO SIGN UP FOR OUR NEWSLETTER AND RECEIVE FREE RESOURCES.

★ ★ ★ ★ ★

PLEASE CONSIDER LEAVING A REVIEW ON
AMAZON IF YOU LIKED THIS BOOK!

TABLE OF CONTENTS

LONG A
SET

The Babe

The babe wanted to fade away from fame. He was well known on the cane farm. The farmers waved each day as they went to a kale sale. But it was ok. The babe was loved and was given many gifts. The babe was given a vase and a fake rake. The babe came to like the cane farm.

The Snake and the Rat

There is a tale of a snake and rat chase. The snake was fast, but the rat was **smart**. The snake planned to make a snack out of the rat. The snake saw the rat was not awake. He made a mad dash to catch it. But the rat was faking. The rat ran to escape his fate. The rat and snake raced in and out of the cane bushes. Finally, the rat tripped the snake into a cave. The brave rat went back to get a snack of grapes and had the best day.

Jake Can Bake

Jake loved to bake cakes and make shakes in his kitchen. His best snack was a snake shaped baked grape. One day, Jake had a plan to make a cake for his **friend** Sam. As he began, he made a mistake. He added too much batter to the pan. The cake was no good. But then, with a little frosting, Jake made the cake into a fun shape. It was just like a cane. In the end, Sam was happy with the cake and gave it a good rating. From then on, Jake knew that he could fix his mistakes.

The Wise Whale

In a spade shaped sea, there was a whale named Lake. He loved to sing tales of run and chase games. One day, he saw a bunch of pale whales trying to race. But they kept making mistakes. Lake had an **idea** and called them over. Lake said that they needed to find their pace and not rush. The pale whales listened to Lake's words so they would not make a mistake. Soon, they were **able** to finish a race. From then on, the whales learned that keeping a good pace is better then going as fast as you can.

The Plane

Yate thought he must be in a daze. Yate **saw** a plane fade into a maze of kale plants. The plane could not be real. Or it was not safe. This made Yate run **toward** the plane by the kale plants. But then he saw Kate, who had a snake by her case. She said that the plane was just a fake. It was made with tape and was used as a prop in a **movie**. The snake was a fake too. Yate was so happy. Yate ate his snack while watching the plane fade back away from the maze of kale.

The Snake Race

Once upon a time, there was a snake named Vane. Vane liked to get out of his cave and into the sun. One day, a snake named Tate told Vane about a fad called snake racing. Vane wanted to race but he was a bit lame. Vane wanted to get fast so he ate kale each day. After many days, Vane was **ready** for the race. When he got to the race, he saw a ton of snakes and even a few apes. It was going to be a hard game to win. Vane got to the line and "...3..2...1... go". He was so fast! The apes and snakes could not catch him! He won. All the other snakes were amazed by Vane's new pace. Vane was in first place.

The fake Race

Sam and Kate had a chase race by a cane tree. Sam was fast, but Kate was **faster**. Sam was **afraid** he'd come in last place in the next race. So Sam made a plan. He put on a fake limp and acted like he had a lame leg. The race **planners** did not suspect a thing and let him start in front of Kate. But as soon as the race began, Sam took off running. He went from the gate, to first place. Kate was shocked that Sam faked a lame leg. Sam felt bad. He made a mistake by **cheating**. He said sorry to Kate. He even gave Kate his winning cane case.

LONG E
SET

The Chess Dog

Pele the dog loved to play chess in the **park**. Every eve, he would bring his **chessboard** and ask other dogs to play for a tasty cheese snack. Pele was a supreme chess player, known for his fast **moves** and quick thinking. Despite his small size, Pele loved to compete. Even humans would stop to watch him play, amazed by his skill. Pele won lots of cheese in his time playing chess.

The Trapeze Competition

One day's eve, Leke and Peve went to compete in a trapeze game. They were both athletes and wanted to **show** off their skills. They worked hard every day, trying to be as complete and supreme as they could be. As they did the **routine**, they were both amazed at how well it was going. The crowd cheered as both Leke and Peve did their best.

The Athletes

Pete and Steve were athletes. They wanted to compete in the extreme sports **scene**. They worked hard every evening to complete stunts. The theme of their stunts was the eve breeze. They had a concrete set of things to do. On the day of the big event, Pete and Steve **forgot** the best snack they had. Cheese! Cheese was a key for Steve and Pete. They walked quickly like a stampede to get cheese. Pete and Steve got some cheese at a store and went to compete. They both won in first and second place.

Queen of the Geese

It was quiet in the days eve. The geese were having a party. One of them was a bit odd. Her name was Beve. Beve was a supreme athlete, able to fly **higher** and faster than any of the **other** geese. She had fun with the trapeze. All the geese loved Beve. Even the children that watched Beve on the trapeze loved her. It was no surprise that she was thought of as the queen of the geese. She was supreme in every way. And every evening, the geese would gather to watch their queen, Beve, perform in the sky.

The Book

Tele wrote a book with a good theme. It was about an athlete who competed in extreme **sports**. The Athlete's name was Pete. Pete wanted to achieve his best win yet. He wanted to win so bad that he did not use his **manners**. One evening, at a stampede competition, he did not say "please" when he asked for his cheese. Gene, the theme park **vendor,** did not like Pete because he did not use his manners. Gene deleted Pete's name from the list of athletes. Pete did not compete because of what Gene did. When Pete asked Gene why he did it, Gene explained. Pete said he did not think what Gene did was right, but he **understood**. Pete used his manners from then on. Tele **wrote** a good book about it.

LONG I
SET

The Tribe

One day, a tribe of mice were tired. They went to take a hike. The mice climbed over rocks and crossed cliffs of ice to rise to the summit. They sat to look at the pretty hills. Then, a vile bird came and tried to snag one of the mice. The vile bird missed. The mice were in a state of strife while they ran to hide. Next, the mice went back to their hive. From then on, they made a rule to never go too far from the hive.

The Best Ride

Mike hopped on his bike and started his ride. The sun shined and it felt nice. He went down the **street** and kept a good stride. It was beautiful and it gave him a smile. He rode past the vine hills and took the **beauty** in live. He came across a tribe of bike riders who were having a jive time. Mike **rode** with them and rode twice as fast. They took a dive into the shady pine trees. Then, they stopped for a rest. Mike took a slice of melon and ate it just fine. The ride was a great way for Mike to get some exercise. This was the best ride.

The Vile Swine

Once there was a vile swine who lived in the Nile. He would dive and eat all the fish he could find. He tried to hide, but the tribe **found** out. They had wanted him gone for while. Mike, a nice guy with a bike that shined, said they should rise up and strike. So they took a stride and tried to drive the swine away. But the swine was too strong and would not **sway**. So Mike and the tribe decided to go on a nile dive and give him a good **fright**. The vile swine, with a bit of a fright, swam away and was never seen again. The tribe all smiled in the end.

The Sight of the Mite

Mike was on a hike and came across a fine site **where** he saw a nice mite. He watched as the mite took a dive into a pile of ice. Mike tried to catch it, but the mite was too quick. It went into the air with a nice stride. The sun was shining **bright.** Mike sat down to take in the beautiful sight of the vine. It twined **around** the pine tree. While he sat, he could not help but smile at the sight of the mite's life and the way it swiped away from him. Mike kept on his hike, grateful he got to see the beauty in such a small mite.

Skating on the Lake

In the **winter** time, the ice on the lake was nice to skate on. Mike would glide along the ice and make dives up and down like a swan. He would shine with pride as he would stride the lake. He tried to better his skills each time. Mike's wife, Kate, also loved to skate. She was not as skilled as Mike, but she was **always** trying to strive for more. She would take her time and make sure each step was precise. One day, as they skated together, the sun started to rise. Mike and Kate liked the quiet.

LONG O
SET

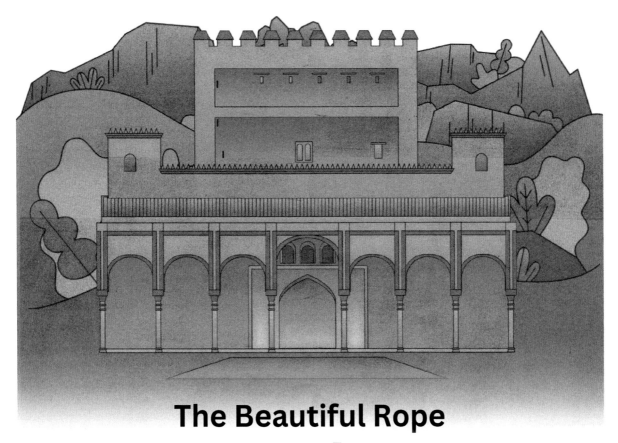

The Beautiful Rope

Once upon a time, in a Roman home, there was a rope made of stone and roses. The rope was alone and had never been used. It was **found** in a hole in the home and was quite odd. People tried to poke and smoke it with fire, but it was as solid as a bone. The rope was close to the dome on top of the home and had a beautiful rose tone. People were amazed and chose to leave it alone. They looked at its beauty and said it was one of a kind, like a work of art from Rome. The rope became a **treasure**, with a scent of roses that seemed to explode with each episode.

Explode!

Once upon a time, there was an egg yoke that **tasted** so good when it was smoked in an grill outside. But be **careful!** If you poke it, it could explode! The yoke was in a scope and had a cone-shaped nose. It was close to a stone rope that was used in a joke. The yoke woke up one day and stole the show with its delicious taste. People chose to smoke it outside, as they did not want it to explode. They used a pole to hold it and a hose to **control** the smoke. The yoke was the sole focus and gave them joy. They felt as if they were on top of the world, just like the yoke in the smoke.

The Scone and the Mole

Once upon a time, there was a broke rodent named Mole who lived in a cozy cove. One cold day, Mole woke up and craved a warm scone. He went out of his dome all alone. As he strode down the path, he saw an open **bakery**. But Mole noted, he had no money. In fact, he did not even have a stone or bone to his name. He felt alone and hopeless until a kind man **offered** to pay for his scone. Mole felt joy. Mole sat down and loved every bite. As he ate, he made a note to always help others in need, just like that remote and helpful man did for him.

A Mole Hole

A big-nosed boy went on a walk by the coast. He **found** a stone cove. At first, he said "nope" when he got close. But his **curiosity** got the best of him. He went to take a close look at the closed stone cove. He saw a mole in a hole. He put his hand inside it and pulled out note. The note read, "Please help me, I'm all alone in here." The boy was filled with hope and wanted to help the mole. He got a rope and pushed it down into the hole. The mole got up the rope. Then, he drove the mole to a remote throne abode.

On Top

Once, there was a girl named Rose who loved to climb ropes and coves. One day, while she was going up a rope in a remote cove, she heard a snap. She quickly realized she had broken the rope. She was now stuck on top of the cove. She felt alone and hopeless. But then, Rose saw a note. The note said there was a secret way down the cove on the other side of the dome. She went to explore the dome and hoped to find a way out. She drove her feet to the dome, but when she got there, she found that it was closed. She looked around and saw a hose that lead to a rope. Rose climbed down and went home.

LONG U
SET

The Cube

Once upon a time, there lived a frog named Duke and a cat named Yule. They were cute friends that liked to comute and play. One day, they stumbled upon a huge cube and went to play a game with it. It was a rubix cube. Duke tried to **solve** it but found it too hard. Yule, on the other hand, was amused by Duke's attempts and watched with a cute grin. Then, they heard a tune coming from a lute. They gave up on the cube and wanted to make some music. They played and **danced** to elude the cube and their **worries**. They saluted their friendship and the joy they had. Together, they had a volume of fun.

Rute's Flute

Rute was a mute girl who loved to play her cute flute. She would spend a lot of time playing, and her music was full of nice tunes. One day, she wanted to **perform** for the town in June. Some people in the town were rude. Rude people sneered, but she did not let the comments fume her. She ruled over her **nerves** and played a beautiful tune. The people were in awe, and even the duke was amused. He said she was the winner and gifted her with a huge mule. Rute was happy and used her prize to buy a new flute made of runes. From that day on, she was known as the flute-playing muse of the town.

Rufus and the Rubix Cube

Rufus the dog was a cute pup with a huge love for puzzles. He loved to play with his crude cube toys. But the rubix cube was a hard thing for Rufus. He tried every way he could think of to solve it. But the cube eluded him. Despite his efforts, the cube went **unsolved**. But Rufus did not make an excuse. He refused to give up. He saluted the cube and refused to lose. He spent time each day to find the right way. After one month, Rufus, amused, defused the cube. It may have been a fluke, but Rufus was still happy.

Rude Dupe

One June morning, the rude mule named Dupe had to commute to a new place. He did not like **following** rules, but he had to. He was used to being left alone in the dunes, but now he had to join the huge herd on the **road**. He accused the other mules of being too cute and not as rude as him. But, as he walked, he **heard** the sound of a beautiful tune from a flute player. He was amused and forgot about his rude attitude. He even saluted the flute player as he passed by. From that day on, Dupe decided to elude his rude acts and be more open to new things.

The Music Master

Mike was an acute flute player. He was always in tune and never missed a chance to use his flute. He was amused by his music teacher. Every day, Mike would commute to the music school and play his crude flute with a high volume. He tried to fuse his skills with his teacher's. He would often dispute his friends about who had the best music. But even so, he knew there was no excuse for not paying tribute to his teacher. One June day, Mike was chosen to perform in front of the teacher. He was **nervous**, but he did not confuse his skills and gave a great flute show. The people were left in mute amazement. Mike felt good to have made a cute tribute to his music teacher.

Dear Friends,

Thank you for choosing our book. I hope that this book serves you and your family well. If you have found value in this book, please consider leaving us a review on amazon. It would be very much appreciated.

Adam Freeman

Here is a suggested order to teach beginning reading skills.

 **Short Vowel Sounds**

 Digraphs

 Consonant Blends

 Word Endings– s, ed, ing.

 Silent E

 **Vowel Teams**

 **Controlled R**

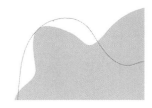

Made in the USA
Las Vegas, NV
17 October 2024

97036751R00024